INTUITIVE
MOON
RITUALS

INTUITIVE MOON RITUALS

Find your unique connection to the power and magic of lunar cycles

LEAH KENT

WILD MOON
press

Copyright © 2021 by Leah Kent

All rights reserved.

No part of this book may be reproduced in any form or by any electronic or mechanical means, including information storage and retrieval systems, without written permission from the author, except for the use of brief quotations in a book review.

The information in this book is not a substitute for professional medical advice; always consult a physician for physical, emotional, or medical problems. Neither the author nor the publisher can be held liable for any loss, claim, or damage allegedly arising from any information or suggestion in this book. In the event you use the information in this book for yourself, the author and publisher assume no responsibility for your actions.

ISBN 978-1-957234-99-1 (paperback)
ISBN 978-1-957234-98-4 (ebook)

Cover and Book Design by Leah Kent

WILD MOON PRESS
www.wildmoonpress.com

*I honor you for exploring and embracing
the beauty and power of the moon.
My heart is full with gratitude for your courage
and willingness to expand, shine, and blossom
into the full radiance of your being.*

let your soul shine

CONTENTS

Finding the Moon	1
Blessings	9
Creating Intuitive Rituals	11
The Lunar Cycle	19
Preparing for Ritual	31

FULL MOON RITUALS

Cord Cutting Release	43
Fire Healing	53
Mandala of Surrender	63

NEW MOON RITUALS

Open to Receive	77
Self-Love Embodiment	87
Spiral Walk	97
Lunar Integration	109
Sacred Stones	119
Lunar Aromatherapy	137
Further Reading	153
Acknowledgments	155
About the Author	157

you are luminous

FINDING THE MOON

Like so many women I know, I suppressed my feminine power for years, trading my own potent mysteries for the socially acceptable pursuit of conformity, productivity and masculine-oriented achievements. Year after year, I ignored my instincts, refused to listen to my intuition, and fell deeper into a state of dissatisfaction and disillusionment.

And then, I broke. I pushed myself along the conveyor belt of other people's expectations until I couldn't sustain the charade. Graduate from a good college? Done. Move in with a sensible partner? Check. Get a steady job in a boring and reliable industry? If you say so. (I picked variable annuity retirement plans).

This required me to override my inner voice, suppress my desires, and continually ignore my deepening sense of indifference. Eventually, all these choices led to a life filled with stress, isolation, and grief. I woke up every morning in my Southern California apartment at 5AM and logged into the phone system at my desk before 6AM, when the financial markets opened on the East Coast.

Cheerfully I answered the phone "Thank you for calling, my name is Leah, how can I help you?" My work required perfection because giving bad information about the client's money and accounts could be near-catastrophic. I also took trade requests from broker-dealers, that left no room for mistakes. It was a dream for the part of me who loved clarity and control, but a slow death for the wild, creative spirit of my true nature.

Even though I appeared successful on the surface, I was coming apart inside. I was living with someone but had never felt lonelier. My body set off all its alarm bells until I couldn't ignore things any longer.

First, it was inexplicable stomach pains. I would crumple in half and go home to sleep for the rest of the day. Then I broke my hand while walking from my car to my office.

Yes, I literally fell off my shoe while walking and landed on a hard, concrete path, fracturing my right hand. The two weeks before my fall, every day at work I'd been silently repeating the mantra "I just need a break!" Looking back, I see how clearly and directly I manifested this accident in the most literal way.

A break is what I wished for, and a break is what I got. My hand was now wrapped in a big clunky black cast, the first and only time I've had a fractured bone. I came off the phones at my insurance company job and was reassigned to several weeks of slow-paced data entry work. At the same time, I was undergoing a dental implant procedure, which meant I could remove one of my front teeth whenever I wanted to.

On the one hand, I saw myself as a strong, independent woman. I was trying to check all the boxes of achievement I'd grown up believing in. I tried to rearrange myself inside so I could fit the mold of everyone else's expectations.

But you can only deny your truth for so long. My life became so uncomfortable, I dropped everything and walked away. I quit, I left, I sold my furniture, and gave everything up. I packed my belongings into a tiny trailer, hitched it to my car, and drove to the desert.

I unloaded everything into a storage unit in Arizona and then boarded a plane for Ukraine for a pilgrimage with my grandmother, to her birthplace in Kharkov. This was my first step off the road that was leading me in the completely wrong direction, and it saved my life.

Walking away from my old life symbolized something deep and true. It was my departure from a straight and narrow path carved by someone other than myself. Sailing down the Dnipro river, drinking vodka with the crew, and learning the Cyrillic alphabet created the ultimate reset I desperately needed.

When we arrived in Odessa, on the Crimean Peninsula, I noticed how many women looked like me. I felt so deeply rooted and connected to my ancestral lineage. This sense of belonging sparked my Heroine's Journey in that moment, and the years-long endeavor to find, reclaim, and integrate the Divine Feminine qualities within me.

This led me to the moon and her magic. As I found the pieces of healing and wisdom I'd been seeking, I slowly forged my personal definition of what it means to be a strong and wise woman, mother, and leader.

My journey was just as circular and looping as the path the moon carves across the sky. I kept coming back to the same places, over and over again, trying to understand each lesson I most needed. Slowly, subtly, the moon's wisdom stitched itself right into my life without me fully realizing it at first.

As I began exploring Tarot, astrology, and witchcraft, it was clear the moon held everything together. She was the pulse beneath it all, a steady heartbeat I could feel in my breath and body. Her cycles were my cycles. Her rhythmic undulations held a powerful key to unlocking my full potential and carrying me into a life of greater contentment and alignment.

I found wise women to share their secrets with me. I read every book I could get my hands on relating to moon cycles and rituals. I developed my own ways to work with lunar energy, creating ceremonies for myself and with a few kindred spirits.

All I knew was the deep inner yearning I felt to commune with the moon and bring her undulating energies into my life. My experience as a moon ritualist is deeply personal and completely rooted in my intuition. This book is a result of my direct experience and exploration with integrating lunar wisdom into my life.

This is what I hope this book can offer for you, too. A guide to support you on your own journey of befriending the moon and embodying your cyclical nature through curiosity, intuition, and direct experience.

In these pages you'll find my rituals, but I know you'll discover how to make them wholly and completely yours. There is no one or right way to bring the moon into your life. But turning back to her shimmering, silvery secrets was so vital to my life's blossoming, so I decided to share what I learned with you.

Reclaiming lunar wisdom brought peace, magic, and sisterhood into my life. It quenched a thirst I could sense but didn't fully understand. Standing around a fire under the full moon, casting slips of paper into the flames, I remembered who I truly am and where I came from.

Allowing lunar energy to animate and guide my life has awakened my intuition, activated my creativity, and provided a clear and flexible structure of ease and joy I can trust in.

Together, we are all children of the moon, guided and influenced by her cycle of ebbing and flowing. By integrating moon rituals into your life, I hope you find the way home to your beautiful, intuitive, feminine self.

the world is thirsting for your light

BLESSINGS

you are a Moon Beam
a perfect droplet of light
ephemeral, radiant
imperceptibly strong

your connection to Source
will never be broken
your light never truly diffused
your true power always accessible

ever-present, you confidently wait
to be uncovered, invoked,
nourished and treasured

your soul spark
the perfect glowing
intensity that is you

you shine, you melt,
you flow and you circle
back to the beginning

trust yourself and the wild magic that lives within you

CREATING INTUITIVE RITUALS

I call myself a 'recovering perfectionist' because I love so much to do things correctly. When I first started exploring moon rituals, I wanted to get everything just right. I followed supply lists to the letter and attempted to time my ceremonies perfectly.

Unfortunately, this also meant I felt stressed and anxious, and if I missed the perfect window, I was disappointed and felt like a failure. But over time, and with the help of many friends and mentors, I relaxed my efforts and flowed more easily with my lunar rituals.

When I began leading Cacao ceremonies in alignment with the moon cycles, I had fully given in to this intuitive approach. On New and Full Moon ceremony days, I would start mixing my cacao brew with pinches of cayenne and cinnamon and listen to whatever wanted to bubble up within me. The warmth of the stove and intoxicating scent of spicy-sweet chocolate brought me deep into awareness of my body, heart, and breath.

I wouldn't try to research, generate, or plan out an elaborate ritual. I just listened and allowed myself to trust whatever insights and ideas would come through. One day I remember receiving a feeling about a purple heart meditation. This was my only guide when I led the evening's ritual.

I created a simple altar with flowers and candles, brought everyone into the circle with a cleansing white light visualization, and then introduced everyone to the cacao. We drank together, sipping the velvety liquid, and then I led the purple heart ritual without a script or plan.

The words came through me as I spoke them into the circle. While I was talking, I received a stirring image of a circle of women wearing gorgeous crowns, each decorated with raw spikes of purple amethyst.

As the ceremony came to a close and we shared our experiences, we discovered three of us received this same image of an amethyst crown. Clearly, we'd been tapping into something collectively, and our energies had gathered around this vision. Everyone was quiet as we sensed the awe-inspiring presence of spirit within this intuitive Full Moon ritual.

This Cacao Ceremony is the perfect example of an intuitive ritual. It's a way of being in a close and direct relationship to your intuition and to the loving energy of the Source, the Divine Beloved, the Universe, All That Is, or whatever spiritual entity you feel connected to.

Intuitive rituals are guided by your inner listening. They're most successful when you allow yourself to follow your heart and your inner voice.

Within this book, you'll find a gathering of simple, open-ended moon ritual templates so you can begin working with these lunar energies in your own way.

Each ritual isn't so much a prescription or set of directions as a warm and open invitation. There are instructions, supply lists, and invocations so you have enough resources to begin. When you feel called to change and add to them, follow that inner calling to move more deeply into your own intuitive realms.

You're living a busy, modern life. It often feels like everything moves at warp speed, and you wonder how to add one more thing to your life. Yet if you're feeling spiritually parched, making even a little time and space for these practices will rejuvenate you from the inside out.

What I hope most of all is to make these rituals accessible, so I've woven these key values into each offering:

1 - Simple Supplies

When ritual is a way of life, you don't need to get hung up on fancy or specific tools. You can create rituals from whatever's right at your fingertips. The natural supplies outside your door, the tools you use every day, and the ingredients you already have in your kitchen. You don't need to harvest wild nettle from a remote hillside to express your mystical, moon-child self!

2 - Time Flexibility

Another barrier to ritual practice is thinking you need hours and hours to dedicate to your personal ceremonies. Regardless of where you are in life's seasons, I know time is a precious commodity for you. While you read through and practice each ritual, please experiment, modify, and adjust things to suit your unique lifestyle. It's always better to start where you are and do what you can. I promise the moon will love and accept you deeply and completely, whether your ritual lasts five minutes or five hours.

Whether you've got a free afternoon or just a few minutes in between the busy-ness of life, this guidebook offers you many ways to incorporate the power and blessings of practicing Intuitive Moon Rituals into your life.

3 - Inclusive and Loving

Most moon books focus heavily on the gender binary between masculine and feminine energy. I appreciate and understand this approach, but I think it's important to offer rituals that see past these confining definitions. The rituals here are fluid, flexible and inclusive in the hopes that anyone feels comfortable working with these invitations.

These ritual practices are deeply rooted in self-love and self-acceptance. I intend for each practice to be uplifting and life-affirming. My greatest wish is that by connecting with the moon, you can cultivate a sacred, nurturing, and positive relationship with your highest self.

Part of the intuitive ritual process is giving yourself the time and space your practices need to evolve and grow. Every time you take these moments out of daily life to drop in deeper with yourself is an opportunity to fall more in love with the delicate dance of sun, moon, and earth. Moon rituals can be a portal to directly access the ancient wisdom of the Earth and your ancestors.

When you feel this buoyant experience of interconnectedness, it brings balance, wellbeing, and contentment. Working with the moon elevates your awareness to that which is so much bigger than the individual. The moon is a living history. It's the same orb all humans before us have gazed upon. Your connection to her weaves you into the infinite tapestry of past, present, and future.

I wrote this book for those who want to work with the moon individually, as a solo practice. But it's also relevant if you want to work with others to create community rituals, in large and small groups. However you practice, the main thing is to follow your inner wisdom because it will lead you to the most aligned and authentic expression available to you.

After each ritual, you'll find three additional tools to deepen your practice.

Ritual Enhancements

At the end of each ritual are suggestions and invitations to take your experience deeper. They're specifically oriented for days when you have more time and spaciousness to sink into your work with the moon and the ritual. This includes invitations for daily practices to sustain and amplify the energy of your ritual work through the rest of the lunar cycle.

Writing Prompts

For most of us, taking time to write and reflect on the ritual we just experienced helps us more deeply integrate any wisdom or transformation that moved through us. You can use these writing prompts if they inspire you, or simply record what you felt, saw, or heard during a particular ritual. If you love this part of the process, consider keeping a separate Intuitive Moon Ritual journal to maintain a record of your notes and reflections.

Intuitive Card Reading Spreads

Tarot and Oracle cards can be a fun and artistic addition to your Intuitive Moon Rituals. If you're experienced with and attracted to card reading practices, there's a three-card spread associated with each of the rituals offered here. Fortunately, there's an ever-growing number of wonderful books on this topic to further support your Tarot or Oracle practice. You'll find my personal favorites in the Further Reading section at the end of this book.

THE LUNAR CYCLE

The moon is a mirror of your own cyclical nature. She is round, ever-changing, and mysterious. Yet she's perfectly reliable in her constantly shifting appearance. She's a luminous paradox of coolness and warmth.

The moon gently yet persistently shapes the world around us. She governs the ocean tides, and her 28-day cycle is the basis for our calendar months.

Humans have long been intrigued by the moon, producing a trove of knowledge, lore, and mystical theories to understand the way she moves and changes through the night sky. The moon is our constant companion. Humans used her light and cycles to develop the first systems for keeping time and marking the changing of the seasons.

I love the enchanting interplay between science and spirituality reflected in the phases. As you study and work with the moon, you'll uncover a swirl of mysticism, magic, astronomy, astrology, and physics playing together.

But you don't need to get overwhelmed by science and precision to welcome the moon into your life. She is just there, out in the sky, fully available to you whenever the alignment is right between her and Mother Earth.

The moon follows her undulating cycle from light to dark and back again with steadfast regularity. Her appearance and disappearance in the night sky is a cosmically orchestrated dance between the sun, the moon, and the Earth. There are beautiful metaphors buried here, secrets about the power and importance of reflection, connection, retreat, and alignment.

As the moon shines and then dims, she seems to breathe, spiraling into the dark of her inner world as she exhales, then sweetly returning to the light again in a full-bodied inhale.

Just bringing your awareness to the moon's journey across the sky is a powerful way to work directly with its wisdom. You can do this as well, by keeping a moon journal for at least one full cycle from New Moon to Full Moon and back again.

You can find a variety of moon journals specific for this purpose or keep your thoughts in a simple spiral-bound notebook. What matters for all these rituals is not the quality of your tools, but the quality of your inner listening and your attention.

In the most basic sense, the moon cycle is a 28-day journey the moon takes around the Earth. It begins with the sliver of New Moon, culminating in the bright Full Moon, and ending with the Dark moon, when none of the sun's light is reflected on her surface. Then, the light returns, and on a breathtaking New Moon evening you see a glimmering arc of silver return.

Bringing moon rituals into your life is a way to slow down and reconnect with your own inner cycle. While I love the simplicity of daily charting and journaling to track the moon cycle, there's power and magic available to you with a deeper ritual practice.

When you start to make space and time for ritual, it can feel overwhelming. You might even feel less likely to observe and commune with the moon phases. This is why I suggest beginning with one or two rituals each month, focusing on the Full Moon and New Moon.

While you move through these pages and explore the rituals offered here, I invite you to always focus on what inspires and works for you. Take this journey at the pace that's good and right for you, in whatever season of life you're walking through. Tuning into this potent lunar energy can happen in sweet, slow baby steps.

If there's one thing I've learned from this work with the moon, it may just be this: slow down. Don't rush. Be with what is. Look up and revel in the overwhelming beauty of your aliveness.

New Moon + Dark Moon Energy

New Moon and Dark Moon are two distinct points of the lunar phase. When I first began my moon journey, I didn't understand this difference, but now I appreciate and honor their unique wisdom.

Dark Moon is when the moon is fully hidden from view, reflecting no light from the sun at all. This is the true end of the cycle, the symbolic death of the light. It's associated with the Crone aspect of the Triple Goddess archetypes and a time of fallow and rest. Dark moon is when you can sneak out into the wilderness, unseen and unknown.

I like to imagine Dark Moon evenings, past and present, for cloaked women to gather in dense forests to practice powerful magic and rituals. These wise women love and appreciate the darkness to protect their anonymity and intensify their spells and blessings.

Dark Moon is a threshold, a moment in time when one thing comes to an end and creates space for something new to arise. Dark Moon is the exhale just before you inhale a fresh, intoxicating breath filled with oxygen and possibility.

New Moon is the first evening that light can be seen in the sky again, the start of the next lunation. When it hangs low in the sky, the New Moon is a brilliant glowing slice of light who always catches my breath. It's fertile and fruitful. I can feel its life force energy condense into such a tiny space, just ready to burst forth.

As you work with these rituals and create your own, I invite you to make notes of what your personal impressions are of these two aspects of the moon.

DARK MOON
Reflection Prompts

- What does the Dark moon inspire within you?

- How do you feel about death and endings?

- Could you practice your rituals more fully in the secrecy of the Dark moon?

NEW MOON
Reflection Prompts

- How do you experience the energy of the first light of the New Moon?

- How do you feel about birth and new beginnings?

- What do you feel inspired to focus on during the New Moon phase?

Waxing Phase Energy

The waxing phase is the 14 days (approximately) between New Moon and Full Moon. During this time, the amount of light reflected by the moon gradually increases, appearing to grow and expand in the sky. For rituals and creativity, this phase of the lunar cycle offers energetic support to nourish new ideas and creative endeavors.

If you're working on something new, it may be easier if you align your schedule with this waxing phase. This can be a positive time for growth, learning, and meeting new people.

For rituals, the strength of the New Moon is typically strongest in the first three days following the Dark moon. These are wonderful days for performing rituals related to articulating your big dreams, setting intentions, and beginning new projects.

Full Moon Energy

Full Moon is the culmination of the growing phase, a time of ripeness and intense power. This is the crest of the cycle, the pinnacle of the light's intensity. The fullness of the moon in the sky is

WAXING PHASE
Reflection Prompts

- What most wants to be nourished within you?

- Which project feels the juiciest and most alive right now?

- How are you growing and shifting within yourself?

FULL MOON
Reflection Prompts

- What feels ripe within you?

- How can you be a conduit for more creative power?

- Where can you expand your capacity for fullness and abundance?

enchanting and alluring. She's radiant in her expansion, filled to her most abundant capacity.

This is a moment for celebration, acknowledgement of how much you've accomplished, and a chance to revel in the brilliance of life.

Filled to capacity, we sense the descent and exhale coming next as we allow this big energy to release and dissipate.

Waning Phase Energy

The waning phase is a time for releasing and letting go of the habits, relationships, or beliefs that no longer support you. As the cycle moves back towards the Dark moon, you can ride this shedding energy to amplify your ability to let things go with ease.

This allows you to bring things to a close and make space for the coming New Moon, when seeds will want to be planted again.

Beyond letting go, I also work with the waning phase to dissolve and transform any patterns, dynamics, or energies causing unwanted anxiety or stress.

WANING PHASE
Reflection Prompts

- What's ready to dissipate and be released?

- Is there something you want to let go or stop doing?

- How does it feel to surrender what no longer works?

Sometimes it feels heavy to just drop something because we still feel its presence around us. If you've experienced this, you may find it liberating to imagine these unwanted things turning into a delicate stream of droplets just floating away, fully dissolved and ready to be recycled into something good and beautiful.

unfurl and expand

PREPARING FOR RITUAL

There are a few useful items for your intuitive ritual journey I recommend gathering ahead of time: a lunar calendar, ritual toolkit, and tools for clearing your space.

Lunar calendar

While I'm all for a spontaneous and intuitive ritual practice, I find it comforting to know when the Dark, New, and Full Moon will land each month. This awareness helps me plan my life and work commitments to align with these energies and to be sure I leave time and space for my moon rituals.

While you don't have to be rigid or overly precise with timing your rituals, ideally you can practice some kind of ritual within one or two days of the key points of the moon phases. To plan for your Intuitive Moon Rituals, mark the New Moon and Full Moon dates on whatever calendar you use most frequently.

Many printed calendars are now marked with New and Full Moon, or you can write it in by hand. If you use a digital calendar, you may need to adjust a setting to add the moon phases or add them manually. If you look online or in specialty bookshops, you can find lunar planners and calendars specifically oriented to astrology and the moon phases. I like to keep a moon phase app on my phone so I can check where we are in the lunar cycle, even if I don't have my planner with me.

If you need to purchase specific supplies for a ritual you're going to explore, make a note on your calendar with a reminder for a few days ahead of time. The more you can set yourself up for spaciousness and ease on the day of your ritual, the more you can go deep into your experience.

In whatever way you choose to explore and develop your moon practice, please be gentle and loving with yourself. There is no doing this wrong. Sometimes the Full Moon will correspond with a day you are sick, have a huge meeting, or the car has a flat tire. Breathe into it and pick things up when you can. If celebrating both New Moon and

Full Moon each month feels like a burden rather than a blessing, let one of them go and then give yourself lots of love and compassion.

These rituals are meant to support, nourish, and fill you up. If something doesn't feel good, surrender and know when the timing is right. The moon will be waiting for you with loving, welcoming arms.

Ritual toolkit

Creating a ritual toolkit is a way to keep all your moon ritual supplies together in one place. This makes it easier to store and care for them so they're ready for the next ritual. If you share your space with others (such as partners, children, or pets) you may want to keep your supplies in a closed box and place them out of reach.

The intuitive ritual toolkit can be simple and meaningful, not overwhelming or elaborate. You may already have lots of items in your life to add to this, or perhaps you're starting from scratch. I tend towards simple, low-key rituals I can create with things I already have around my house. This removes any barriers or resistance I might feel about doing a ritual in the first place!

Your toolkit should be a reflection of you and include things that bring you joy and inspiration. There's no need for any specialized or expensive tools, but it's certainly fun and meaningful to gather totems, tools, and trinkets that make you smile while you're practicing your rituals. Physical objects absorb and carry the energy of your sacred work, making them more and more meaningful as your intuitive practice blossoms.

I believe having tangible objects to focus on can help you better access your unseen connection to the Divine. I've only suggested tools I personally work with on a regular basis and have found to be helpful and enjoyable.

For the moon Rituals in this handbook, these are the tools and supplies to gather together:

- Pens / Pencils / Markers
- Paper
- Candles
- Matches
- String / Ribbon
- Incense
- Smoke cleansing bundle / Palo Santo
- Tarot or Oracle cards
- Bell or Chimes
- Essential Oils

- Crystals / Stones
- Ceramic or fire-safe bowls

Please remember all of this is optional, and you can be flexible with these suggestions. It's likely you already have the pen, paper, candles, and matches. So, if you were to purchase just three special items, I would suggest starting with a smoke cleansing bundle or incense stick, an essential oil, and a crystal.

I love keeping all my ritual tools together. You can do the same in a box, a drawer, or even a small bag of some sort. Just take care to ensure you wrap things to prevent breaks or spills, and tuck them away somewhere safe and out of reach from unwanted hands or eyes.

For specific essential oils and healing crystals to work with, you'll find a basic reference guide at the end of the book. This includes a limited range of favorite oils and crystals, along with specific suggestions for using these energies to support your ritual work.

Clearing your sacred space

Whether you're practicing your rituals in your home or outdoors, it's always beneficial to create a clean, clear energy in your physical space. In the most literal sense, it's helpful to tidy and clean up the area where you'll be doing your ritual so you can keep your attention focused on your intentions.

On the energetic level, space clearing makes room for the energy to unfurl and expand, within and around you. This spaciousness helps you feel present and aware that you've moved out of the everyday and into a moment of sacred purpose.

When done with your full attention, clearing and cleansing your space can be simple and doesn't have to take more than a few moments. In keeping with simple and accessible rituals, you can use the following three ideas just about anywhere. You can perform them one at a time or combine them. Circumstances, preferences, and time constraints usually determine what works for you on any given day.

If you discover you love this part of your Intuitive Moon Rituals, you can incorporate these clearing techniques more frequently into your life. Tending to your space can become part of your daily or weekly routine to support a healthy and vibrant energy in your physical surroundings.

Sound Clearing

The vibration of sound moves energy in your physical space. Similarly, chanting and singing create healing vibrations within your body, producing a healthy flow of vitality. This means almost any sound can help you clear your mind, body, and space before a ritual.

When using sound in a room, you could try shaking a rattle, beating a drum, clapping your hands, or ringing a bell. Any of these methods will clear the space. Walk around your space in a circle, making sounds and spending extra time in the corners of a room where energy is prone to get stuck.

To clear your physical body with these types of sounds, sit in a comfortable position, close your eyes, and allow the sound waves to move through you and stir your energy. Set an intention for anything negative or unnecessary to be carried away by the sound waves.

When using your voice to clear your energy, you can hum, chant, or sing. Sitting comfortably and singing the single syllable chant of "om" three or four times is a brilliantly simple yet deeply satisfying method of hooking into the energy of Spirit.

Water Clearing

Water infused with essential oils is a refreshing way to clear the energy of your body and home. You can purchase room and body mists already mixed or make your own. It's as simple as dropping some oil into water and using a bottle with a spray top.

Some classic essential oil scents used for creating a fresh energy are Eucalyptus, Peppermint, Cedar, Juniper, Cypress, Lemon, and Orange.

With spray bottle in hand, lightly mist your body or spritz into your physical space. As with the sound clearing, walk in a circle, spraying a little here and there, paying particular attention to the corners of the room.

You could find or create your own mantra, blessing, or invocation to go along with your water clearing. You can speak it out loud or silently repeat it in your head. While you clear the air with the water, you can visualize the energy in the space shifting and clearing, imagining negative or stagnant qualities evaporating with each water droplet.

Smoke Clearing

Lighting an herb bundle to cleanse your space and body is a traditional and effective way to create sacred space. This smoke can be quite potent, so a little goes a long way!

I invite you to be mindful and intentional about working with herb bundles that align with your ancestral lineage or the land where you currently live. Whenever possible, it's ideal to burn something you've grown yourself, or have purchased or received from a local farmer or herbalist who follows sustainable and organic growing practices.

Where I live in North America, I usually work with cedar, lavender, or sage bundles. Rosemary and juniper also make delightful herb smoke bundles. If you responsibly gather or harvest your own herbs, you can blend them together and make your own unique combinations.

If just thinking about growing, gathering, or purchasing fresh herbs sounds stressful, skip all of this and buy what you can, where you can! Along with these herb bundles, you can use an incense stick for a similar effect.

Incense comes in a vast assortment of scents and blends. When choosing incense for a clearing ritual, look for high-quality ingredients without artificial fragrances, which can have a negative effect on the health of you and your space.

To clear your physical space, walk around the perimeter with your smoke cleansing bundle or incense and allow the smoke to move through the entire space. You can use the smoke to clear your physical body as well. Wave the bundle or incense gently around yourself and allow the smoke to accumulate a bit, then walk through it.

Smoke has the added spiritual effect of rising into the sky as it dissipates, a clear symbol of sending negative or unwanted energies up to the heavens to be transformed and dissolved, gently and easily.

> *"each place is the right place*
> *the place where I now am*
> *can be a sacred space"*
>
> *~ ravi ravindra*

FULL MOON
RITUALS

CORD CUTTING RELEASE

Each of us has energetic cords connecting us with others in ways that are healthy, and occasionally, in ways that aren't so healthy. These are sometimes called etheric cords or 'ribbons' of energy and they connect you to people, places, animals, objects, situations, and past events.

As you work with the Full Moon to release and make space for new dreams to take root, you may find certain patterns, relationships, or habits no longer serve you.

A gentle, loving cord-cutting ritual is a symbolic way to disentangle yourself from a person or situation that no longer serves you. By approaching this ritual with respect and love, you can create a healthy separation to reclaim your personal power and energy. You can think of this as recalling your power back to you so you can experience a greater sense of wholeness in your life.

Even if you have negative emotions around this situation, including a sense of guilt or obligation, try to stay centered on your true intention to bring greater health, growth, and wellbeing to both you and any other involved parties.

Gather materials

- Paper
- Pen
- String
- Scissors
- Photo of yourself

Pre-ritual grounding

Start by standing with your feet planted firmly on the ground, preferably barefoot. Do this outside if you're able to. Because you're intending to move a lot of energy with this ritual of releasing, take the time to tether your personal power and boundaries closely to Mother Earth for her help and support.

Imagine roots growing out of your feet, deep into the ground below you. Take a series of long, slow, deep breaths as you repeat this sacred mantra:

I am here

As you repeat the mantra, feel yourself filling up with a bright glowing light from head to toe. See all your energy being drawn back into your body. Feel yourself gently and lovingly retrieving anything that's been misplaced or lost from your soul-body. When you feel ready, open your eyes and begin the rest of the ritual.

Prayer of invocation to start the ritual

> *Beloved Guides, I invite you to be present with me here tonight, to support and guide me through this process.*
>
> *Allow this ritual to be a healing for my highest and best good.*
>
> *I ask for your blessings and grace as I gently cut these cords with love and forgiveness for myself and all other beings.*

Ritual writing

Start by writing down what you'd like to let go of. You can do this in a few short sentences or write out several journaling pages. The most important element is to let your truth out onto the paper.

If you're thinking about a significant or heavy situation, try to take it on in small pieces or layers. You can start with taking on a single element or facet of any particular person or issue.

For example:

> *I'm ready and willing to release any lingering negative energy hanging onto me after getting laid off from my job. I want to move forward with positive energy and surrender the doubts, resentment, and sadness I've been holding onto about this situation.*

Next, take the photo of yourself, roll it up like a scroll, and tie one end of the string around the photo. If you don't have a photograph of yourself, you can write your name down on a slip of paper instead.

Take your paper or journaling pages with the situation you're releasing, roll it up, and tie the other end of the string around it. As you hold the two ends of the string in your hand, state your intention or prayer out loud. You can repeat the script below as is, alter it, or create your own.

Releasing prayer

> *Spirit, Guides, and Divine Love, I'm open to receiving your blessings and I call on you to help me heal, release, and surrender all that which no longer serves my higher purpose.*
>
> *As I cut this cord, let it be a symbol for bringing my energy back into my body.*
>
> *Let it help me release and let go of any energy that doesn't belong to me. As I cut these cords, surround me with Divine healing light and bring my energy into alignment with love, trust, and acceptance.*
>
> *I offer gratitude for your blessings and assistance.*

Cutting the cord

Lay out the cord and use a pair of scissors to cut the string connecting your image from the writing that symbolizes the person or situation you're releasing. The power of this ritual comes from you visualizing physical cords being severed. Your intention energizes and activates the ritual, so do what you can to hold the intention for this to be a gentle, healing, and loving process.

Keep love and kindness at the forefront of your mind as you perform this ritual so it may have the desired effect of supporting you to move forward from wholeness, rather than staying connected to anger, resentment, or other negative feelings.

Completion

Once you've cut the cord, it's time to dispose of these ritual elements with care. If you have the option to do so, you may burn the cord, photo, and paper all together. You can do this in a fireplace, fire-safe vessel, or outside. Always use great care and caution when working with fire and avoid burning traditional photographs inside as they contain plastic, and the smoke could be harmful.

An alternate method is to submerge the ritual materials in water. Hold an intention for the energy to transfer to the water and then pour it outside or into a larger body of water. The paper and cord have symbolically lost their power and can be disposed of with your household garbage.

Your ritual is complete when the cord has been cut and the materials have been discarded carefully.

Ritual enhancement (*optional*)

To enhance this ritual, you can take a cleansing and purifying bath. This symbolizes the fresh start and renewal you're working to create with the cord-cutting process.

As you bathe, imagine the soap and water helping to heal and complete the releasing energy created by your ritual. When the water is draining out of the tub, see and feel it carrying away any negative or stagnant energy.

INTUITIVE CARD READING

Pull three cards before, during, or after your ritual to support your gentle cord-cutting release. This three-card reading invokes the elements of love, letting go, and personal empowerment to help you deepen your ritual.

As you sit with the cards, allow the energy of self-love, patience, and trust to guide you through your intuitive interpretation of the message being offered.

1 - Release

Clarity around exactly what needs to be released at this time. Guidance for identifying the actions and energies that support this releasing for the highest and best good of all involved.

2 - Love

Wisdom and insight about the qualities needed to move forward and release the attachment to this situation with love and compassion for myself and others. Guidance and insight to help practice self-acceptance on the healing and releasing journey.

3 - Power

How the choice and willingness to release will contribute to the empowerment of all involved. The strengths and benefits that may blossom as a result of completing this healing release.

CORD CUTTING
Reflection Prompts

- Did you notice any resistance to this releasing ritual?

- How does your body feel now, compared to before the ritual?

- What new awareness, clarity, or insight came through during the experience?

- Having completed this ritual, do you notice any new areas needing this same attention to more fully release and call back your power?

FIRE HEALING

Fire is the ultimate transformational healing tool. The power of the flame can take almost anything and reduce it to ashes and rubble. The purpose of a fire element healing is to wholly and completely shift the energy of a relationship, belief, or situation.

The Fire Healing ritual helps you release and let go of anything that no longer serves you. It could be a limiting belief, an unhealthy habit, or an energy-draining attachment.

Drawing on the releasing energy of the Full Moon and performing this ritual when the moon is bright can amplify your intentions and support the healing of the transformation.

Set the intention for your transformation to be fully supported, and these negative attachments will be carried away as the light of the moon dwindles and wanes.

Gather materials

- Paper
- Pen
- Candle
- Fire-Safe vessel
- Smoke cleansing herb bundle or Palo Santo sticks
- Matches / Lighter

Pre-ritual grounding

Before a powerful release, it's important to draw your energy in, restore any power leaks, and reclaim your sense of wholeness.

With a short visualization, see yourself calling back any energy that may have been left behind at different points in your life, recent or from years past. Set the intention that all your power and soul energy is gently and lovingly returning to your body, integrating into your being easily and peacefully.

Know that calling back your energy in this way does no harm to anyone else and is an act of love for all involved.

After you breathe deeply and lovingly through this meditation and process, imagine releasing any energy not belonging to you. Deliver it safely to the hands of Spirit for safekeeping or transformation. Know that letting go of this energy is for everyone's highest and best good.

When you feel ready to do so, slowly bring yourself back into your body, gently open your eyes, and continue with your ritual.

Prayer of invocation to start the ritual

Divine Beloved, I come to you and offer you that which no longer serves me, asking you to carry it away to be peacefully transformed.

I offer this energy to your safe and loving hands, letting it return to the Earth, to be re-formed into something fresh and vibrant.

My heart is open and ready to receive your blessings, love, and support. I call on the Spirit of Fire to nourish, support, and guide me through this ritual.

Heart of the ritual

The heart of this ritual is to become clear about what you're ready to release and then symbolically offer it to the fire for healing and transformation.

Because not everyone is comfortable with fire or has a safe environment to perform a ritual with an open flame, I will offer safe alternatives for each step.

The first step is to write down what you're offering for healing and release. This can be as simple as a few words or a longer written description. You can write it in a way that feels like a prayer, or it can be direct and to the point.

Here are some things I've worked on in past rituals for inspiration:

- I release my fears, worries, and self-doubts

- I release my belief that I must look a certain way to be happy

- Dissolve and transform my impatience with finding my soul's purpose

- Gently release my unhealthy attachment to the relationships I've consciously chosen to complete

Whatever you choose, write it down on a small index card or a piece of plain paper. For ritual work, I like to write on something more special than thin white printer paper, like cream drawing paper or thick watercolor paper, and I typically use colorful pens or metallic markers.

Once you write the releasing wish on paper, say a simple prayer as you offer it to the flames. Here's an example prayer:

> *Divine Beloved, please help me release this energy with ease, compassion, and love.*

If you're able to do so, you can burn the paper by lighting it with a candle or match in a fire-safe environment. This could be a large cooking pot, ceramic bowl, outdoor fire pit, or fireplace.

One alternative is to wave the paper through the smoke of incense or a smudging wand. I love using Palo Santo sticks for Fire Healing rituals because they have a lighter scent and are less messy than herb bundles, like sage, cypress or lavender.

For a completely fire and smoke-free ritual, use an aromatherapy cleansing spray and spritz it symbolically onto your paper. You can make your own with a few drops of essential oil from smudging herbs like sage, juniper, cypress, diluted with water in a small spray bottle.

Regardless of the exact method you choose, the intention and energy are the same; you're asking the divine to help you release and surrender.

As you offer your paper to the flames or smoke, take several deep breaths to assist the releasing process. Feel into your body and see if you notice any sensations arising.

If there is tension or resistance, breathe gently and lovingly into those places. Know that whatever amount of healing takes place with this ritual is exactly perfect for you right now. You may not experience a total and complete release or transformation with a single ritual.

Honor yourself for the willingness to show up, stay open, and be wonderfully vulnerable in this moment.

Completion

To complete the ritual, carefully dispose of any ashes or paper that remain. Ashes can be returned to the soil and paper can be buried as well. Or you can soak your paper in water, offer the water to the Earth, and the paper to your recycling bin if you're comfortable doing so.

Releasing work can feel draining and emotionally charged, so be sure to nourish yourself deeply after this ritual. Stay hydrated with lots of water or soothing teas.

Clear as much time and sacred space as possible following this ritual so you can follow whatever intuitive urges you experience for rest, reading, time outside, or perhaps gentle walking.

Ritual enhancement (*optional*)

You may find journaling about your experience helps you integrate and process whatever came up for you during the ritual. To enhance and amplify the power of this releasing ritual, consider a follow-up journaling practice for a certain number of days following the Fire Healing.

If you noticed an area of your body seemed to carry tension or resistance during the original ritual, you could place your hands on this same spot each morning or evening to continue allowing and supporting the release.

This is an effective way to tap into your innate self-healing abilities. It's also a gentle and accessible form of self-care and self-love that supports deep and lasting transformation following this ritual.

INTUITIVE CARD READING

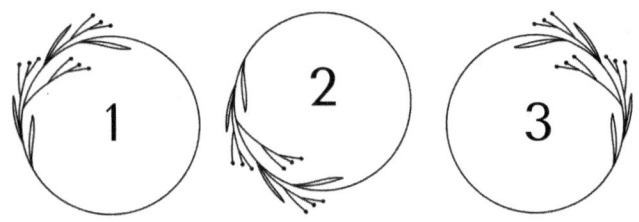

In any transformational process, you encounter resistance and obstacles on some level. This reading helps illuminate those obstacles and offers insights into what's most needed to guide the healing process along. As you do this reading, offer yourself compassion, time, and space to allow the intuitive messages to deepen.

You may feel called to leave the cards from this reading out for several days. This can spark further understanding of the ongoing healing process you've started.

1 - Obstacle

Anything currently interfering or blocking me from experiencing the healing I seek. Obstacles and blockages I may not yet be aware of that I should consider or explore to support the healing process.

2 – Healing

Energies, themes, and even mantras that will support the healing process. Clarity for knowing exactly where to focus my energy and attention throughout the coming weeks on the healing journey.

3 - Balance

Guidance for moving forward towards a state of harmonious balance through the healing process. What energies I should be mindful of to maintain a healthy balance in the present moment. How to sustain and amplify the effects of the healing work I'm embarking on in the present and carry them into the future.

FIRE HEALING
Reflection Prompts

- What does the spirit and energy of fire feel like for me?

- How alive am I willing to let myself be?

- What ripples do I want to send out into the world?

- What's being integrated and woven together?

- Can I sense the Full Moon's support with this releasing ritual?

MANDALA OF SURRENDER

When something feels too heavy, overwhelming, or hard to bear, it's time to turn things over to a higher power. By surrendering your concern to something bigger, you open an emotional, mental, and spiritual space where you previously felt blocked and burdened.

The heart of this ritual is to build a symbolic portal to symbolize the release and transformation of your concern or burden. To do this, you construct a circular mandala to serve as a temporary sacred place to perform your surrendering ritual. The mandala represents a gateway where you can deliver your concern to the healing and powerful embrace of the cosmos and infinite source energy.

Building your mandala is a slow and nourishing act of creativity and brings you deeply into your body. It's both a meditative and tangible way to open the lines of communication between you and Spirit. The process of arranging the mandala elements offers you time and space to slow down and become open to seeing new solutions and opportunities around the burden you're ready to surrender.

Gather materials

- Candle
- Matches
- Essential Oils
- Tumbled stones / rocks
- Quartz crystals
- Flower petals / leaves
- Other small objects to add to the mandala

Pre-ritual grounding

Before beginning your ritual, consider if there's a particular deity you want to work with. If so, you can call on them by name to make the ritual feel more personal and intimate. In most traditions, moon deities are female goddesses, but there male moon deities exist in some cultures.

The Roman goddesses Diana and Luna are both associated with the moon. In the Greek pantheon, the moon goddesses are Artemis and Selene. In the Celtic lineage she goes by Rhiannon and to the Aztecs, she is Metztli.

Take time exploring the lunar gods and goddesses connected to your lineages and notice if you experience a spark of knowing or curiosity about any one in particular.

If possible, get more fully grounded by cleansing your body. You can take a luxuriously slow-paced bath filled with salts, flower petals, and essential oils. If you only have time for something quick, opt for a ceremonial shower or symbolically wash your hands, feet, or face.

Whichever option you choose, do it with a sacred intention to clear and purify your energy, washing away negativity, stagnation, and anything else needing to be released.

After the cleansing, anoint yourself with an earthy essential oil like Patchouli, Sandalwood, Jasmine, or Rose. These scents help you connect with the divine and with your inner wisdom.

Prayer of invocation to start the ritual

*Divine above, I come to you in full surrender.
I give myself over completely to your loving
arms and all-knowing, all-seeing embrace.
I am open and ready to receive your blessings.*

Heart of the ritual

To begin the ritual, find a flat surface where you can arrange your mandala. You can use an altar, a table, a large tray, or perhaps a spot outside. Wherever you decide to arrange the mandala, think of yourself spinning a golden thread of light around you as though you're in a sacred healing bubble.

Create a soothing ambience in your bubble with devotional music, a few candles, and perhaps a favorite elixir to drink. Choose something in alignment with the seasons, like an iced herbal tea in the summer or a hot spiced drink in the Fall or Winter.

With your materials gathered together, begin laying out the objects you've selected to form a circle. You can create one or more rings of singular objects, or you can mix things together. Traditionally, mandalas are designed with a sense of symmetry to mirror your intention of creating greater balance in your life.

> *"I bow to the infinite teacher within and open myself to the infinite source of wisdom and creativity within me."*
> *~ ong namo sacred prayer*

As you place petals, stones, and anything else you're using for the mandala, feel into how this symbolizes the round, receptive nature of the moon and Mother Earth.

If you're using flowers, imagine yourself letting go of your burdens and attachments with each petal you remove and place in the mandala. Whatever is holding you back or causing you discomfort, let it melt into these petals and these stones as you arrange them in ever-widening circles.

Try alternating the petals and crystals to create patterns that feel pleasing and luscious to your eye. It can be quiet and monochromatic with a focus on texture. Or it can be a riot of color and diversity.

Follow your intuitive urges and creative inspirations as you build your circular portal. Trust yourself to know when the Mandala is complete, remembering it's wonderful to err on the side of less being more. Simplicity can be blissful.

When your mandala is complete, it's time to write down the thing you're surrendering to your chosen deity or higher power. You can write it on a small slip of paper, phrasing it as a prayer or request. Then fold it up and lay it down in the center of your mandala.

Speak whatever is on your heart to the Divine. Say it out loud as if you were talking to a trusted confidante and feel the energy releasing from your body and spirit as the words flow from your mouth. Think about directing energy into the center of your mandala and visualize it being sent up and down to the ground, above and below, so it can be transformed.

By letting this energy and resistance melt away into the heart of the mandala, you're making space to welcome new solutions, creative healing, and Divine blessings into your life.

Prayer

*I release my attachments to the
outcomes my ego craves.*

*I pray to you for strength and to
provide a clear path for me to follow.
I surrender. I surrender. I surrender.*

Completion

Close the portal created by your mandala with the power of your intention. You could symbolically spray it with a smudging mist, wave it with sage smoke or incense, or even pass your hand over it several times for closure.

When your ritual is over, you can leave the mandala out to enjoy its beauty and to be reminded of your commitment to releasing and staying open to Divine blessings. For the releasing prayer on paper, the preferred method of completion is to bury it outside, perhaps with a few flower petals from your ritual.

If this isn't an option, you can burn the paper safely or wet it with water to create the feeling of completion. When you are ready to dismantle the full mandala, cleanse your crystals with a scented mist or under the light of the next Full Moon.

Ritual enhancement (*optional*)

Strengthen your relationship with the deity or goddess you choose by making offerings to them as an expression of your gratitude, faith, and trust in their power. Having surrendered your situation, you can focus on pouring love into your relationship and channel with the Divine.

I used to feel overwhelmed by choosing an offering that was good enough or perfect. But my anxiety had me miss the point entirely, of simply making a heartfelt gesture infused with my love and intentions. You can make any of these offerings, daily or weekly, with or without a specific altar.

These are examples of simple, lovely, heartfelt offerings:

- A fresh flower
- Small bowl of fruit or seeds
- Sing a song
- Feed the birds or animals near your home
- Small dish of salt
- Light a stick of incense
- Small dish of honey
- Bowl of fresh water

INTUITIVE CARD READING

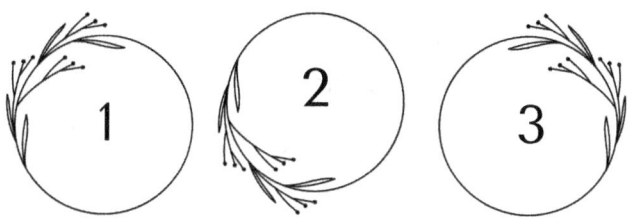

Pull three cards before building your mandala or at the close of your ritual to gain deeper insights on how and what to surrender. This reading focuses on the connection between you, the situation you want to surrender, and the unseen blessings woven into your experience.

While you sit with these cards, take time to slow down and listen deeply to whatever intuitive wisdom you receive. Cultivate the energies of trust, openness, and flexibility as you intuitively interpret the message the cards are offering.

1 - Higher Power

The energy of the divine or deity influencing the current situation or question. The qualities and characteristics of my higher self that will support me moving forward powerfully on my current path.

2 - Surrender

Clarity and insight about where I'm truly ready to release and surrender in this situation. What wisdom and strength I'll need to draw on to stay committed and open to the ongoing practice of surrender.

3 - Blessings

The Divine Blessings being offered related to the current situation. Anything I need to see or hear to be reminded of my connection to the Divine, Spirit, and Source.

MANDALA OF SURRENDER
Reflection Prompts

- When you surrender, where do you feel a weight being lifted?

- Do you notice any attachments to your own suffering under the weight of this burden?

- Who can you become when you stop holding onto this situation or thing?

- What has this ritual shown me about freedom?

- Having made this space, what juicy, audacious dreams are making themselves known?

NEW MOON
RITUALS

OPEN TO RECEIVE

This ritual is centered on manifesting true, soul-aligned abundance. It's easy to get wrapped up in materialism and confused by the ego when you hear the word 'manifesting.' Rather than tuning into your intuition and soul's voice, you might start focusing on a list of things you think will fill a void of longing and not-enough-ness.

Buddhists call this state of being the 'hungry ghost' because no matter what you feed it, the creature wants more and more. It can never be sated.

In the Open to Receive ritual, you're expanding your capacity to call in what will truly nourish you, and receive your deepest desires without attachment to specific outcomes. It's a tender, gentle way to expand your soul's ability to accept the Universe's gifts and practice letting go of expectations. The underlying intention is to experience a balanced flow of both giving and receiving.

The potential of working with the New Moon for this ritual is to make space for love, support, and strength where you previously experienced doubt, lack, or wanting.

Gather materials

- Bowl
- Pen
- Paper
- Incense
- Essential oils

Pre-ritual grounding

To center yourself for this ritual, you will activate your capacity to receive by generating energy in your Root chakra. Standing with your feet hip width apart, begin by taking several deep breaths, allowing the air to fill your lungs to capacity.

Bend your knees slightly and place your hands on your hip bones. Slowly begin rotating your pelvis to make gentle circles. Feel energy flowing into your pelvic bowl and loosening up any stiffness or resistance you may feel here.

Allow your body to tell you what it needs to add here. Imagine spiraling this energy up to your torso, gently twisting and rolling through the back.

If it feels good, raise your hands up into the air while you circle your hips in a gentle hula-hooping motion. As you make these undulating rolls and circles, repeat this simple mantra to yourself, silently or out loud:

I am Open. I am Open. I am Open

Prayer of invocation to start the ritual

Beloved source energy, I blissfully flow
in your river of abundance and love. As I release,
I make space to receive. I am willing and open to
receiving the support and nourishment you provide.

I call on you to help me create space for receiving
your gifts and expand my heart's ability to see all the
ways I am blessed. I come to you in gratitude.

Thank you for all you've given
and for that which I have yet to receive.

Heart of the ritual

Begin by selecting a favorite bowl you'll use from now until the next Full Moon for this ritual. It will need a place to live, such as your dresser, a spot on the kitchen counter, or an altar if you have one. It doesn't have to be very large, and it can be quite simple. In fact, I love using a plain white porcelain bowl for this ritual.

Place the bowl on the ground in front of your feet and light a stick of incense in your hand. As the smoke wafts, move it in a series of circles over the bowl. Speak a prayer of consecration over the bowl. Let the words flow forth and come from the heart.

You can begin with this prayer or create your own:

> *I bless this bowl as a symbol*
> *of my ability and willingness to receive.*
> *I am open to the gifts and miracles*
> *that flow into my life.*

> *I am open to the mystery of abundance.*
> *Let this smoke carry all that no longer serves me,*
> *releasing these energies into your loving hands.*

Placing the incense somewhere safe to continue burning, take the bowl in your hands and infuse it with love. Imagine white and golden light traveling through you into the bowl.

Take a moment to write three things you're grateful for in this moment on small sheets of paper. Anoint each piece of paper with a drop of an essential oil or perhaps give each one a light kiss. Fold them up and place them into the bowl.

Now you can take the bowl to the spot where you'd like it to continue receiving blessings from now until the Full Moon. Each day, or as often as you remember, write down a blessing you're grateful for and place it in your receiving bowl.

At the next Full Moon, you can lovingly release the slips of paper by burying or burning them so they can return to the Earth and the Divine.

Do this with love and feel deeply that by letting go, you're making room to receive again. Like breathing, this movement of giving and receiving is a natural, healthy, and nourishing cycle.

Completion

This could be an ongoing ritual or daily practice. However, on the day you first perform the blessing of your receiving bowl, you can close your ceremony by making an offering to the Divine to express your gratitude for the blessings you've already received.

A lovely way to do this is to light a small chapel candle or even a birthday candle to seal your intention. Anoint the candle by rubbing a drop of essential oil associated with abundance, such as Orange or Ylang Ylang. Then light the candle near the receiving bowl and allow it to burn all the way down.

Ritual enhancement (*optional*)

To go deeper with the ritual, take this opportunity to create tangible space by releasing physical objects from your home that no longer nurture you or inspire joy. This amplifies your intention of opening yourself to receive abundance by literally clearing things out of your physical environment.

Rather than a complete clutter-clearing project, try approaching this with tiny, doable steps. You can begin by gently selecting just one or two objects to release every day. You could do this right before you write your daily blessing for your ritual receiving bowl.

As you drop off your possessions at a donation center, give them away, or recycle them in a way that feels most appropriate, bless the objects with love and a prayer such as:

> *I release you with love so
> you may continue joyfully on your journey.*

> *I trust that as I let you go,
> I make space for new blessings to arrive in my life.*

INTUITIVE CARD READING

Like a lightning rod, we can conduct more energy when we're properly anchored and grounded. This reading keeps your energy focused on being grounded and rooted, so you have the strength and stability needed to give and receive what's needed to grow, expand, and thrive.

1 – Peace

The energy to help me access deeper levels of forgiveness for myself and others as a pathway to greater freedom and ease. Perspectives, symbols, or elements that will help me sustain my intention to move forward with a sense of inner peace.

2 – Grounding

The actions or themes keeping me deeply connected to Gaia and Mother Earth. The message I need to hear to create a solid and loving foundation, so I feel safe to open my heart.

3 – Open Heart

New perspectives to help me experience greater trust and willingness to be vulnerable in this situation. What's needed to open myself wider to fully receive the blessings, love, and acceptance being offered by the Divine, Goddess, and Source Energy.

OPEN TO RECEIVE
Reflection Prompts

- With my hand on my heart, what does my inner voice want to share?

- What do I most want to open myself to receiving?

- Where do I hold fear and resistance to opening and being vulnerable?

- How does it feel in my body when I say "I am Open, I am Open"?

- Are there gifts being offered in my life that I've been overlooking?

SELF-LOVE EMBODIMENT

What better seed to plant than deep self-love, acceptance, and compassion? In this ritual, you're cultivating a whole-hearted experience of yourself by celebrating the union of your body, mind, and spirit.

This is a sensory ritual meant to align and integrate your physical, emotional, and spiritual self. It's also an invitation for you to step into the full range of your power and possibility.

You are here to live out your soul's purpose. You're allowed to take up the space you need to express your creative gifts and make your magic in the world.

I began working with this ritual to help unravel the limiting belief that I was just too much and therefore would only be loved and accepted if I could hide and shrink the unwanted parts of myself. This painful dynamic undermines your natural talents and gifts. It mutes your power, squashes your creativity, and keeps you stuck.

You can include this ritual in your moon practice regularly and frequently. The moon is a nurturing ally who can help you shed these layers of self-doubt and replace them with beliefs that allow you to blossom and flourish. By aligning this ritual with the New Moon, you can ride the waxing energy of growth and step into your full, radiant brilliance.

Gather materials

- Jojoba or another carrier oil
- Rose or other essential oil *(affordable rose oils are typically pre-diluted with carrier oils like jojoba)*

"Be kinder to yourself.
And then let your kindness flood the world"

~ pema chodron

Pre-ritual grounding

You need to claim your space and tie into your connection to the Earth before this gorgeous ritual. To begin, lie down on the floor or even outside directly on the Earth. Breathe deeply into your back, drawing your awareness to the way the air expands through your ribs with each inhale.

Feel how supported you are. Notice every point of contact between your body and the Earth below you. Remember, even when you're not lying down, this feeling of full body support is available to you.

Stretch your limbs gently. Lift your hands over your head, stretching long and wide. Do the same with your legs, feet, and toes, lengthening to claim every centimeter of space available to you.

Make slow, wide circles with your arms and legs as if you are making snow angels. Imagine by doing so, you activate a glowing circle of golden energy around your body. This is your space.

Stay with this grounding experience for as long as you desire. When you're ready, gently roll to one side before carefully lifting yourself to sitting and then standing.

Prayer of invocation to start the ritual

*Thank you for this amazing body
and experience of life.*

*My heart is open and ready to step into the
powerful gifts you've bestowed upon me.*

*I call on you for support, blessings,
and healing so I may fully
embody and express my Divine purpose.*

Heart of the ritual

The deeper purpose of this ritual is creating a love-drenched sensory experience to generate energy and fullness in your body. You will engage the sense of touch, smell, sight, and sound through a sacred full-body anointment with a nourishing oil.

To engage both touch and smell, use a scented body oil for this ritual. You can use a pre-mixed product or make your own by adding several drops of an essential oil to Avocado or Jojoba oil. I prefer Rose scent for this ritual for its high vibration and energetic qualities of love and compassion.

As you rub the oil into your hands and begin the ritual, set the intention you are blessing your body with Divine Love. Start with your left foot and massage the oil lightly into your toes, heels, and ankles. Continue anointing one side of your body: legs, belly, and then your arm and shoulder.

Symbolically anoint your throat, forehead, and the crown of your head which are associated with your Throat, Third Eye, and Crown Chakras. Next, continue down the other side of the body, starting with your arm to your back, and then down the other leg to the foot.

While you're anointing yourself, stay open and relaxed through any surges of energy or sensations as they arise. Breathe into discomfort or emotions bubbling to the surface and know that releasing, including tears, is a healthy and natural expression.

If you notice your body resisting anything, or you feel the urge to hide, even from yourself, breathe love and acceptance into these parts of you. As you continue communing with your physical body in this way, you can invoke your preferred divine being or deity in a prayer mantra spoken aloud or repeated to yourself silently.

I am here. I am love. I claim my space.

Completion

Part of self-love is self-nourishment. Simple as it is, water is one of the most powerfully symbolic ways to nourish your body. To complete this ritual, slowly and lovingly drink down a tall glass of clean, cool water.

As you drink the water, use the experience to complete your ritual. Know that with this ceremonial libation, you're honoring the moon and nourishing yourself with the healing power of water. Chant or speak a prayer such as this one:

Divine Beloved,
I know I am nourished through you.

I love myself completely, just as
you love and accept me completely.

May this water and oil hold and keep
our connection as I walk my Divine path.

Ritual enhancement (*optional*)

Just as you moved your body to begin this ritual, so will movement help you fully integrate the experience of your anointment. This is sometimes called Ecstatic Dance, a form of spiritual movement to unleash your divine, creative energy.

Find a rhythmic piece of music like a Kirtan chant or other devotional music you find resonant and moving. Allow yourself to sway, move, and dance in whatever way comes up for you. The theory behind Ecstatic movement is freedom of expression. There are no steps and no need to worry whether you're doing it right.

You're just releasing and surrendering into whatever shape your body desires to take. Allow this divine, source energy to move through you, so all that's left to do is dance with it.

Dance for as long as it feels good and as often as you like. This dance of spiritual surrender is a moving way to bring harmony to your body, mind, and spirit.

INTUITIVE CARD READING

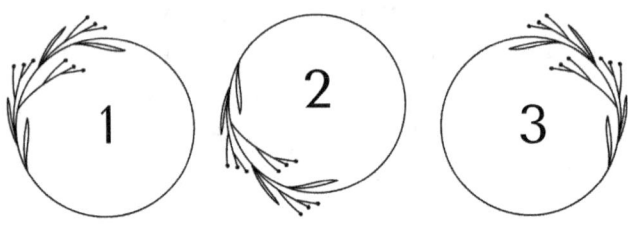

Mirroring nature's wisdom, the cards in this Soul Blossoming spread match the three key phases of a growing plant. All living things follow this same arc, of being planted, sprouting, growing, and then returning to a resting phase, or being composted in some manner.

As you pull the cards for your reading, see yourself as the incredibly alive being that you are, enjoying your human experience of growth and unfolding.

1 – Soil

The cosmic and energetic energies governing my current potential for growth. The current environment and circumstances influencing my life and this situation.

2 – Root

Where to focus my energy to tap into my Source connection and Divine guidance. How to nourish myself and draw out my unique, sacred gifts and strengths. Energies to draw on to keep me grounded and supported through any coming transitions.

3 – Bloom

How I can open myself to growth, receiving, and expansion. What best supports deep soul-care and self-care right now. What energy supports me with self-love and self-acceptance so I can rise up and be seen.

SELF-LOVE EMBODIMENT
Reflection Prompts

- What do I need to rekindle my inner warmth?

- How can I more fully and deeply love myself?

- Where are the dark corners where I make myself wrong?

- What will I forgive myself for?

- When I love myself, what creative gifts become more available for my work and play?

SPIRAL WALK

Tracing the lunar cycle in a walking meditation is a powerful way to deepen your inner listening and connection to the wisdom of the moon's rhythms. By physically tracing a circle or spiral with your whole body, you can sense the inner shifts that occur through this orbital movement.

You can create this ritual as a spiral, walking in and out towards a center point. Or you can set it up as a large circle, symbolically marking the key points of the moon phases. Meditative walking has a long, rich history with our ancestors, who connected deeply with the energy of the earth below their feet.

For a New Moon ritual, you can take a sacred intention or dream with you into this ceremony, visualizing your wishes taking root and flourishing as they travel the spiral with you.

Gather materials

- Candles
- Stones
- Flowers or leaves
- Paper
- Pen

Pre-ritual grounding

Tap into the energy of the Earth by planting your feet on the ground and standing tall. Imagine your feet are sending roots down deep into the earth, giving you life, nourishment, and stability. Bring your hands into a prayer position in front of your heart center and feel yourself deeply loved and supported by the Earth.

Now drop your head down to your chin slightly and imagine a cord of light is flowing from the crown of your head, connecting you to the full, radiant power of the Universe. See this light filling up every part of your body with love, joy, and pleasure and know this is your unbreakable connection to Source.

For the rest of the Ritual, know you are open to receiving abundance from the Earth and nurtured by the energy of the Universe.

Prayer of invocation to start the ritual

*As I walk this sacred spiral,
I call on the moon and the Divine Beloved
to listen to the whispers of my heart and
support me as I call in that which I desire.*

*I trace this circular path to open my heart
so it can more fully receive that which is for
my highest and best good.*

*As I carry and speak my soul's deepest wishes,
I am grateful to you for your
unending gifts, blessings, and wisdom.*

Heart of the ritual

You can perform this ritual indoors or outside, making your circle or spiral as small or big as needed for the space you have. Arrange a line of stones, leaves, or flowers to mark the path you'll walk during the ritual. At the center of the circle, place a candle in a safe container to symbolize the creative fire and provide a focusing point for your intentions.

Make your path large enough to walk two or three times around the circle or spiral, and place a stone or other talisman at four points to represent Dark/New Moon, First Quarter, Full Moon, and Last

Quarter. You may want to draw or print an image of the moon in each of these phases to place at these points around the perimeter of your path.

With your sacred spiral built, spend a moment gazing at the candle and drop within to hear what your heart most desires to take into the ritual. It could be a specific dream, wish, or intention, or perhaps it's a more symbolic and overarching feeling you receive.

As you become clear on what dream or wish to take into the spiral, write it on a small piece of paper and hold it between your hands. Slowly and mindfully, start the path at the New Moon point to signify the beginning of this journey.

In silence or while chanting or singing, walk to the First Quarter and notice how it feels to imagine your wish growing and expanding along the way. Continue on towards the Full Moon, continuing to amplify this feeling of your dream blossoming.

At the Full Moon point of the path, imagine your dream in full fruition. Everything has come together in a magnificent way, as good or better than you hoped.

Keep that feeling with you as you move forward, slowly walking onto the Last Quarter point of the spiral. Notice how it feels to effortlessly integrate this dream into your life and find its way out into the world. Then imagine gently releasing your fulfilled desire after coming full circle, therefore making space for new dreams to take root.

You can repeat this process of walking around the circle to deepen your experience. Or you can journey with more than one wish during your ritual.

If you're walking in a spiral form, you can move towards the center point with the waxing energy, reaching the symbolic Full Moon candle, and walk back outwards with the waning energy.

Completion

When you feel complete with the walking meditation, close your eyes and visualize your energy moving through your body to imprint the wisdom of this ritual fully into your consciousness. Imagine growing roots deep into the Earth to draw up love and wellbeing to flow through your body. Take the piece of paper inscribed with your intention and feel how it's become infused with the energy of this spiral ritual.

Notice what you feel inspired to do with this sacred wish. Does it feel right to light it in the central flame to send the wish up to the cosmos? Or perhaps you feel moved to tuck it into a small pouch and place it on your altar or carry it with you for this moon cycle.

If you have time and it's safe to do so, you can leave the center candle burning to further intensify the power of the ritual you've created.

For an outdoor ritual, you may choose to leave the circle or spiral you've created for a few more days as a reminder and offering of your dreams and wishes. Trust the magic you've created has generated a strong and nourishing energy in your ritual space you can access and tap into anytime.

Ritual enhancement (*optional*)

If you have more time and spaciousness to work with this ritual, you can take this work to an outdoor location where you can more fully commune with the land, plants, and animals.

Depending on the season and where you live, follow your intuition to select a secluded spot where you're unlikely to be disturbed. This ritual works wonderfully in a forest, by the shore, in the desert, or in a sheltered woodland.

You can respectfully incorporate natural elements of the landscape into your ritual, such as tracing your spiral path in the soil or arranging fallen twigs to mark your circular outline.

When you make the spiral larger, it expands the space between each point of the moon phase, providing you with more time to meditate and visualize the energies of growth and releasing in the ritual.

INTUITIVE CARD READING

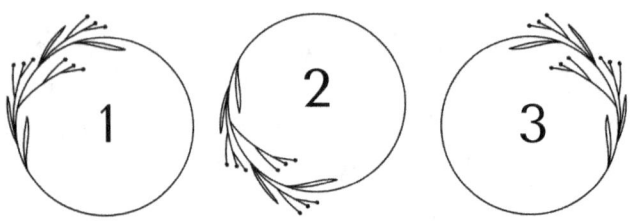

Carrying your dreams around the circle is an act of commitment to bringing them into reality. Along this journey of creation and manifestation, you'll be called on to trust the process, soften your expectations, and nourish yourself and the budding idea that's taking root.

With this reading, you can gather insights and open to further wisdom on how to cultivate and sustain those aspects of the coming lunar cycle.

1 – Trust

What energies will support me in cultivating greater trust in myself in the current situation. Which inner strengths can I draw on to stay rooted in my vision and trust my own abilities to bring them into a physical manifestation?

2 – Soften

What needs to be healed or released in order to support me moving forward and creating this vision. Where can I surrender my attachments or let go of what no longer serves me to make more space for my desires to manifest?

3 – Nourish

The qualities and energies I need to embody and practice to be in alignment with my vision. Themes and perspectives to nourish and tend to my vision, as I call it forth into reality. Key elements to keep my spiritual, emotional, and mental energy in balance while I manifest this desire.

SPIRAL WALK
Reflection Prompts

- As I walk the circle, do I notice any insights about each phase?

- How does it feel to physically carry my dream around the sacred spiral?

- In what ways do I feel loved and supported by the Earth?

- In what ways do I feel loved and supported by the moon?

- Do I sense a difference between walking to the center of the spiral compared to walking back out again?

LUNAR INTEGRATION

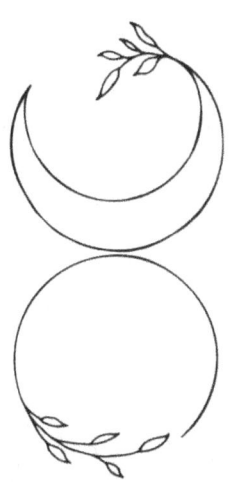

choose the path of joy and illumination

YOUR LUNAR JOURNEY

The wisdom and magic of these rituals grows more potent and nourishing with time, experience, and practice. At first, you may feel uncertain or self-conscious about how to create and move through the rituals. But over time and with an open heart, you'll find your way and build your sense of confidence.

If you make a loving and spacious commitment to these rituals, the moon will show up to greet you. Like any relationship, you'll receive what you put into it, with a true reciprocal flow of energy and attention between you and the moon.

To integrate your moon rituals into your life is like building any new habit. You'll want a plan, or at least a clear sense of how you could incorporate these sacred moments into your life. Ideally, you can set a regular time for your ritual practice, as closely aligned with the lunar cycle as possible.

I understand you might have a full life with a calendar booked out with plans and commitments. As you get started with your practice, I recommend starting with achievable plans that feel sustainable and possible. Where can you find an hour to yourself, either on the New Moon or the day before or after it? This is where being flexible with the precise day and time of your rituals will help you show up.

Understandably, it's challenging if the Full Moon falls on a busy Monday or New Moon overlaps with a vacation or work trip. Nobody is asking you to be perfect or do it a certain way. Even if all you do for one month is look up and notice the moon is there, ebbing and flowing like always, it keeps you connected to your practice.

It's the consistent habit of spending time with yourself that activates the magic of welcoming the moon into your life. She reminds you that sometimes you need to rest, and other times you need to shine brightly and stand fully in your infinite power.

To help you get started with your moon rituals, you can try one of the following plans or map out your own.

3-Month deep dive

For the next three months, work through all six of the rituals in this book. Try each of the New Moon and Full Moon rituals in this book, which entails doing a ritual every two weeks. Enter all six of your ritual dates in your calendar, aligning them as closely as you can to the New and Full Moon each month.

At the end of this three-month cycle, you'll have a better idea about what rhythm works best for you. If it was challenging to show up for two rituals each month, you might prefer to try once a month instead. Then you can focus on either the New Moon or Full Moon rituals for the next few months.

6-Month exploration

For a more spacious and gentle rhythm, do one ritual each month, taking six months to move through each of the rituals in this book. Following the path of the lunar cycle itself, I suggest starting with the New Moon rituals for the first three months, followed by the Full Moon rituals.

This path allows you to become familiar with each of the rituals and notice your own connection to the Full Moon and New Moon energies.

6-Month deep dive

If you have the time and passion to do so, commit to a six-month plan with a Full and New Moon ritual each month. You'll repeat each ritual twice and perform twelve rituals in total.

With this approach, you can adapt and customize your rituals according to your intuition. For example, when you repeat the same ritual, change one or two things the second time and make notes on how the ritual felt the same or different. Every time you engage in your moon rituals, you have the opportunity to learn something about yourself and your connection to the lunar cycle.

12-Month journey

A significant but doable commitment is to plan a full year of moon rituals. Depending on how the lunar cycle falls across the calendar, this typically means there will be 13 lunations. If you're doing one ritual each month, you could focus just on the New or Full Moon. This allows you to repeat the same ritual several times, providing plenty of time to refine, change, and personalize each one based on your inner guidance.

If you prefer a deep dive approach, do the same ritual for three months in a row. This sample plan is a jumping off point, and I encourage you to create your own unique schedule based on what resonates most with you.

January - February - March - April
New Moon: *Open to Receive*
Full Moon: *Cord Cutting Release*

May - June - July - August
New Moon: *Self-Love Embodiment*
Full Moon: *Fire Healing*

September - October - November - December
New Moon: *Spiral Walk*
Full Moon: *Mandala of Surrender*

In this pattern, the rituals are loosely connected to the solstices and seasons of the Northern Hemisphere. For example, the Fire Healing rituals align with the full sun of the Summer and the Mandala of Surrender corresponds to the shedding energy of the Fall.

You can follow this structure or cycle through the rituals intuitively, checking in that week or day to see which one feels the most helpful, nourishing, and useful in the present moment. In the beginning, you could alternate between New and Full Moon rituals in any pattern that works best for you and your life.

However you decide to approach your practice, pay attention to what feels good. You might notice this as specific sensations in your body, or a powerful image or word that comes to your mind. These are all signs of your intuition communicating with you, guiding you towards the best ritual to meet your innermost needs.

Your ritual plan can stretch you outside your comfort zone, but it shouldn't be so intense or overwhelming that you end up avoiding or resisting it completely. Moon rituals are a time for replenishing your soul and spirit. They're never meant to be a burden you associate with stress and anxiety.

Personalizing your rituals

You are your own expert on how the moon cycle and lunar magic work in your life. As you try on these rituals and reflect on these invitations, be sure to change the rituals to suit your environment, your schedule, and your interest. By working with these ceremonies while listening to your inner wisdom, you'll naturally make them your own and weave your unique talents, interests, and skills into their foundations.

Keep a moon ritual journal to make notes about how you set up your rituals and what worked best with each one. Being a moon ritual scientist simply means recording what you did and reflecting on what worked and what you'd like to do differently next time. As you try new things, you'll develop a completely customized and just-right moon ritual practice that brings you home to yourself.

Especially when you're working outside, it's a good idea to ask the land permission before you proceed and to ask it for guidance on where to set up your tools. Incorporate a land acknowledgement if you know you're standing on an unceded territory of an indigenous tribe, for example. By honoring and respecting these traditions, you can bring in more consciousness and awareness to your rituals.

Add your own poems into your ritual experience and sing songs if that's what you love to do. Make noise, drum the Earth's heartbeat, and light more candles. There are no limits to how you set up your rituals and infuse your uniqueness into these sacred ceremonies.

Follow those threads that light you up inside, for this is exactly how these moments are meant to feel: the most alive version of you, expressing yourself with joy and love.

SACRED STONES

MOON RITUAL CRYSTALS

Early in my ritual journey, I felt drawn to the power and magic of Earth's sacred stones, the gems and minerals buried in the soil. Over time, I've grown even more respectful and mindful of these treasures, so I can be sure I'm working with tools that have positive and uplifting energy.

With the growing interest in crystals, there are more choices than ever before and navigating these options can get quite overwhelming! As with everything offered here, I believe in starting small and following your intuition.

Rather than following other people's suggested meanings about what power a crystal might contain, choose stones you love and notice how you feel inspired to work with them.

Along with visiting crystal shops and metaphysical stores for these crystals, you can incorporate stones you find in your immediate surroundings. Like harvesting any natural item from the Earth, ask permission before taking anything out of its home and honor these sacred gifts.

Some of my most beloved stones came from a wide, quiet beach in Rhode Island, where I spent a day in deep ritual and reflection. This was a time in my life of grief and deep inner work. That windswept morning, I felt adrift and lost about which way to move forward.

Standing at the rocky shoreline of a spot called moonstone beach, I felt immediately drawn to the luminous, sand-worn white stones scattered as far as I could see.

With my heart filled with respect and gratitude, I lovingly and gently found 13 'moon stones' that seemed lit from within. Smooth as velvet, each one fit perfectly in my hand and I felt sure I could take them with me.

Later I learned about the power of 13 as a sacred goddess number, and I started working with these stones while I pursued my trainings in energy healing and women's circle facilitation. I arranged my moon stones on altars and carried them with me to classes and gatherings. Years later, I still work with them and feel their energy keeping me connected to this transformational chapter in my life.

The crystals I've gathered in this guide are typically easy to find and reasonably priced. It's likely they'll come in a range of sizes and styles such as tumbled stones, points, or clusters. You're also likely to find lab created or altered stones.

Aura crystals, for example, have an iridescent coating created by heat treating the crystal and applying a mineral layer to the surface. Synthetic and heat-treated crystals can minimize or diffuse the potency of the crystal for this kind of ritual work.

On the other hand, a man-made stone may be more sustainable than harvesting gems from the Earth in disruptive ways, so follow whatever path feels right for you. If you're unsure about the source of a crystal, most shop owners, whether online or in person, are pleased to answer your questions and help you with your selections.

The qualities and properties I've listed with each stone are based on my research from a wide range of sources and my direct experience working with each crystal. If you discover a kinship with these crystal friends, you can keep a dedicated journal to make notes about new stones you choose to incorporate into your ritual practices.

AMAZONITE

Inspiration, Balance, Self-Expression
Chakras: Heart, Throat

Amazonite is a captivating stone with the ability to bring the sacred masculine and divine feminine into balance within your subtle energy body. Supports communication, non-verbal expression, and remembering your connection to the Divine.

AMETHYST

Protection, Purification, Intuition, Confidence
Chakras: Third Eye, Crown

Helps release old patterns and therefore lift yourself toward a higher vibration. Opens the crown chakra to supports connection with the divine, soul healing, and spiritual growth. Possesses a peaceful energy to support meditation and developing your intuitive abilities.

BLACK TOURMALINE

Protection, Grounding
Chakras: Root, Sacral

A ridged black stone, the deep black tourmaline absorbs negative energies, acting like a constant cloak of protection. With potent grounding forces, jet black tourmaline dissolves anxious vibrations, making space for positive energy to nurture the soul. Tourmaline contains electrical properties that are activated by rubbing the stone, so you can draw on this power during your grounding and healing rituals.

CLEAR QUARTZ

Healing, Amplification, Intention, Meditation
Chakras: All (Root, Sacral, Solar Plexus, Heart, Throat, Third Eye, Crown)

Clear Quartz is the mother stone, the most flexible and all-encompassing crystal to work with. Look for clear stones, as they have a higher vibration and greater ability to amplify your intentions. Use for any healing purpose and with any moon rituals.

CITRINE

Abundance, Balance, Chakra Cleansing
Chakras: All (Root, Sacral, Solar Plexus, Heart, Throat, Third Eye, Crown)

A hard-working crystal known to transform and clear negative energy. Excellent to place in any room in the house as an energy filter. Citrine is a wonderful stone to wear or carry for protection as it can absorb negative energy.

JADE

Stability, Prosperity
Chakras: Root, Heart

Excellent stone for rituals revolving around growth and abundance. As an abundance stone, it can amplify your vision and help your creative endeavors come to fruition. Jade supports stability in your life by supporting and nourishing harmonious relationships.

RAINBOW FLUORITE

Grounding, Harmonizing, Clarity
Chakras: Heart, Crown, Third Eye

With stripes of green, purple, blue, and sometimes yellow, this stone represents bringing different energies into harmony with one another. Supports connection with the earth in a grounding way along with mental order and clarity.

ROSE QUARTZ

Self-Love, Compassion, Self-Esteem, Romance
Chakras: Heart

Helps open your heart to unconditional love, both from yourself and others. Powerful for releasing negative emotions (anger, jealousy, resentment) to make you more receptive to positive and loving energies. Carries high energy but is calming and soothing.

SELENITE

Clarity, Balancing, Serenity, Peace
Chakras: Crown

Closely associated with lunar cycles and the divine feminine, this milky, translucent crystal is named after the Greek moon Goddess, Selene. Frequently cut into wands and towers, selenite supports balanced energy, clarity of thought, and focus. Selenite can be used to cleanse the energy of other crystals and physical spaces.

SMOKEY QUARTZ

Transformation, Grounding
Chakras: Root, Solar Plexus

A powerful stone with grounding, earthy properties. Effective at helping transform dreams into reality, perfect for visioning and intention setting. Facilitates connection with intuition and spirit guides.

SHUNGITE

Protection, Purification, Centering
Chakras: Root, Solar Plexus

Shungite activates all 7 of your main chakras. This black to silvery stone is used to detoxify the body and rid the mind of negativity. Shungite is a must-have for people with difficult and uncontrollable emotions. It allows for light to fill the body and negativity to be removed.

Sourcing your sacred crystals

You can trust that your intuition will lead you to the right stones, both when you're purchasing a new one and when you're deciding what to include in a particular ritual.

When I visit my favorite metaphysical shop, I feel an almost gravitational pull towards a particular section or shelf and then discover an exquisite stone I've never heard of before. Other times I'll go intending to find a specific thing, yet leave with something completely unexpected instead.

Once I'm there, in front of a shelf or tray of crystals, one or two will practically leap into my hand right away. Even if I take the time to keep looking, nine times out of ten, I end up taking home the first stone that jumped into my hand.

The common thread in these experiences is the way I follow my intuition and trust the process as I'm selecting my sacred crystal companions. Staying open and therefore detached from specific outcomes is an excellent spiritual habit, and choosing crystals is a very low-risk way to practice this powerful state of being.

Trust your initial impressions and know there's no such thing as a wrong crystal. Even if there was, you can always gift it to someone, pass it on, or return it to the Earth if it's not working with your energy.

Another aspect of the selection process to consider is finding a soul-aligned source for your crystals. I love supporting fellow small businesses with my crystal purchases, whether it's in person or online. When you're getting started with crystals, I suggest purchasing them in person if possible.

If you're not able to visit a physical store, there are online boutiques specializing in high quality and ethically sourced stones and gems. I recommend placing small orders with different vendors so you can understand their quality and service before making any larger purchases. And when you find an online vendor who feels like a great soul match, don't be afraid to ask questions or let them know what kinds of stones you're looking for.

Cleansing and charging crystals

After you've purchased your crystals, cleanse them so they'll be ready to use with your healing and rituals. These cleansing ideas work to charge your crystal and infuse it with your energy as well. Typically, I use one of the following methods.

- Place under the light of the Full Moon for a few hours in a moonlit window or outside.

- Soak or rinse the stones in a saltwater mixture. Salt can corrode some stones, so alternatively, you could bury the stone in a small bowl of salt without the water. This can last anywhere from a few minutes to a few hours.

- Visualize a bright, white light encircling and clearing or charging the energy of your crystal.

- Harness the power of sound vibrations to cleanse your crystals with bells, chimes, or a singing bowl.

After the initial cleansing, you can clear their energy on a regular schedule or whenever you feel intuitively guided to do so. Cleansing and charging at each Full Moon is thought to infuse your crystals with beneficial energy.

It's a good practice to cleanse your crystals after someone else has handled them or after you've completed a specific ritual and now want to use the stones for another purpose.

Infusing crystals with prayer

When speaking your prayers during a ritual, hold the crystal in your hand and imagine it becoming charged with the power of the ceremony. This is like energetically programming a crystal to carry and radiate a particular vibration or healing quality.

When the ritual is complete, the crystal will still carry the energy and vibration of the prayer you spoke. By keeping this crystal with you it can continue to radiate your intention like a beacon of light energy.

If you're unable to carry the crystal, you can instead keep it out in the open, so you see it often. This could be on a formal altar or simply your dresser, nightstand, or bathroom vanity. The most effective practice is to place it somewhere you'll see it often to help you amplify your prayer's intention.

Crystal mandala

With crystals, more is often better, as they can vibrate together to generate increased healing powers. You can create a sacred charging station by arranging a circle of crystals all pointing toward the center.

Placing objects at the center, such as a written mantra, sacred object, or talisman, allows them to receive the positive energy of the crystals.

I typically arrange this crystal grid or crystal mandala with quartz points which can focus the energy of the crystal and send it out in a healing beam. A simple and effective crystal grid is composed of six evenly spaced clear quartz points. You can add additional crystals, but this basic version is effective and a perfect way to experiment with this concept.

Sacred stone jewelry

An enjoyable method for carrying the healing properties of a crystal is to wear it on your body as a ring, bracelet, necklace, or earrings. For maximum effectiveness, it's thought to be more powerful to wear a stone that makes direct contact with your skin. Beaded jewelry, like prayer malas, may have a greater healing effect than stones set in silver or other metals, for example.

You can align your jewelry choices with whatever intentions you're manifesting or ideas you're releasing. If you're looking for an all-purpose crystal jewelry wardrobe, Citrine is a lovely choice as it can filter negative energy. Wearing sacred crystal jewelry is like walking around in a healing bubble of light.

Crystal moon bath

When you're in a soft, receptive, and open state of being, crystals can do their work at a deeper level. That's why a crystal moon bath is such a juicy and sensuous addition to a ritual.

Select a few crystals in alignment with the intention of your ritual. You may choose to take this sacred bath either before or after the ritual. Typically, you would take a bath before an intention-setting ritual and after a releasing ritual.

Arrange the crystals around the tub in a way that suits you or feels intuitively aligned. Placing them at the four corners of the tub or in a circle around you is a simple way to begin. If you have a few stones that won't be bothered by the water, you can place them in the tub with you. Hard, nonporous stones, like quartz and amethyst, work well for these rituals.

As you soak in the warm water, set an intention for the healing energy of your crystals to amplify the effects of your ritual bath.

LUNAR AROMATHERAPY

pleasure is your body's sacred wisdom

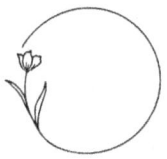

MOON RITUAL SCENTS

The element of scent has a stronger connection to memory and emotion than any of your other senses. You can harness this same power by bringing essential oil aromatherapy into your ritual practices.

You can incorporate scent into nearly every step of your intuitive rituals, from beginning to end.

Whether you're starting a fresh endeavor at the New Moon or creating your Mandala of Surrender at Full Moon, using a scent to remain focused on your intention and desired outcome is a luscious and sensual way to amplify your ceremonies.

Like all other aspects of your moon rituals, you can trust your intuition to lead you to the scents and essential oils that support you best. At one point on my lunar journey, I worked with essential oils daily, using them morning, noon and night to keep me connected to the rituals and work I was focused on.

I rubbed oils on the soles of my feet, carried solid scents in my work bag, and ended each evening by anointing myself with the oil I was working with that cycle. My friend and mentor made delicious blends I kept on my dresser as a sweet-smelling apothecary.

When I decided what scent to work with each cycle, I would open the dark brown bottles of oil and smell each one. I just noticed how I felt with each one and trusted myself to find exactly what I needed. I loved how the scents had been lovingly blended by my friend and given fun names like Expansive Journey and Joyful Heart.

Over many months of working with essential oils, I discovered a curious phenomenon. I noticed an essential oil smelled amazing and magnetic to me when I started working with it. Over time, I'd sense that I was ready to move onto working with a new scent.

A few weeks or months later, I'd revisit the previous essential oil, and it would smell completely different! When I asked my friend about this, a trusted intuitive and healer, she said it's a common effect she sees in her clients. Our higher selves know when we're done working with a particular oil, and our vibration is no longer a match to the frequency of the scent. The oil hadn't necessarily changed, but my perception of it had noticeably shifted.

It's a gentle reminder to lean deeply into your intuition when selecting essential oils to build what I call your lunar apothecary. You can work with single-scent essential oils or in combinations you intuitively feel drawn to. In my experience with oils, you'll feel attracted and inspired by what will best support you for the intention or project you're focused on at the moment.

A few words of wisdom about working with essential oils:

If you have known allergies or sensitivities, exercise caution or consult with a physician before using essential oils. Stop use of any oil immediately if you experience an allergic reaction. Do not ingest essential oils. Pure essential oils should be mixed with a carrier oil, like jojoba, rather than applied directly on your skin.

LUNAR ESSENTIAL OILS
Correspondences

CLEARING + CLEANSING
Cedar   Sage
Juniper

NEW MOON
Ginger   Patchouli
Orange   Cypress
Jasmine

FULL MOON
Bergamot   Tea Tree
Rose   Ylang Ylang
Sandalwood

Energetic properties: Clearing and cleansing oils

Before beginning a ritual, you can cleanse the air and your body with one of these essential oils. Each of these herbs has traditional healing properties associated with releasing negative energy and connection to Spirit. They can be used alone or in combination with one another.

CEDAR

Cedar brings balance and steadiness to your Spirit and encourages connection between Earth and Heaven. It's used for purification rites and to help bring dreams to reality. Cedar is especially effective in calling on ancestors and guides to be present during rituals.

JUNIPER

Juniper helps remove obstacles between you and the Divine and, therefore, clears the pathway for experiencing enlightenment and inner vision. The scent is uplifting and opens the heart, mind, and spirit before meditation and rituals. Juniper has protective properties to prevent negative energies from entering the home, body, spirit, or mind.

SAGE

Sage is a sacred herb that helps integrate Spirit with everyday life. It has cleansing and purifying properties that aid in both healing and protection. Sage is an earthy, grounding scent that helps you feel rooted before performing other rituals and ceremonies.

Energetic properties: New Moon oils

New Moon is a time for beginnings, creativity, and manifesting desires. This outward energy can be very yang, masculine, and action oriented. However, the action and transitions associated with this phase can stir up feelings of apprehension, anxiety, or insecurity.

In order to work with both sides of this New Moon energy, the oils suggested here are both motivating and calming. These scents can help release blockages and allow the desired transition and outcome to take place. Other suggested oils help you cultivate a sense of openness and enthusiasm to welcome new experiences and situations as they emerge.

GINGER

Ginger has a sharp, crisp fragrance, creating a feeling of drive and action. It can help overcome procrastination and inspire you to move forward with your intentions and creative projects. You can apply ginger essential oil mixed with a little jojoba oil or shea butter to the soles of your feet to cultivate a sense of courage and grounding. Ginger is a bright scent that supports joy, peace, and happiness. This oil is thought to be effective with attracting money and abundance.

ORANGE

Citrus scents, particularly Orange, Mandarin, and Tangerine, carry uplifting and optimistic properties. Use Orange to aid transitions by bolstering your emotional vitality. This scent can help you release negativity and, in its place, call in confidence and courage. The uplifting quality of Orange attracts divine blessings and abundance.

JASMINE

An intense floral scent associated with the energy of attraction, seduction, and love. Jasmine is an excellent scent for gaining clarity and manifesting your desires. It has calming properties, helpful for easing fears, stress, or anxiety that may be stirred up when you're intentionally creating a change or transition. Jasmine flowers are sometimes called moonlight of the Grove, making it a perfect oil for moon rituals when the air is cool and dark.

PATCHOULI

This earthy, grounding scent is associated with fertility, abundance, and love. From a spiritual perspective, Patchouli helps nurture your connection to your soul purpose and Divine path. It is a sacred oil that inspires you to action and make strides towards realizing and manifesting your dreams and desires. This scent has a masculine energy for supporting action and momentum.

CYPRESS

The balancing and grounding properties of Cypress effectively support decision-making. It instills a feeling of inner strength and aids in calming the mind. By reducing anxiety and uplifting the spirits, Cypress supports easy, natural transitions. It offers strength and compassion with its warm, spicy scent and encourages you to trust your inner wisdom.

Energetic properties: Full Moon oils

With Full Moon being a time for surrender, the oils selected here support transitions and releasing energy. Working with soothing and calming scents helps you melt into your releasing work with more compassion, love, and patience.

BERGAMOT

Bergamot carries the qualities of balance, joy, and peace. It has an uplifting and optimistic scent to bring emotional vitality to transitions. It helps release the need for control and helps you stay open to new situations. To aid in releasing and surrendering work, Bergamot helps clear negative mental energy and brings joy to the soul.

ROSE

Rose has the highest vibrational frequency of all essential oils. It can help support the transformation of grief and loss because it helps magnetically attract joy and love to the heart. Rose is particularly well-suited to calming the stress of releasing attachments for both situations and relationships.

SANDALWOOD

Sandalwood is associated with harmony, peace, serenity, and unity. It helps release attachments to worldly goods and other material outcomes in a gentle and loving way. This scent helps you see beyond the ego and to see your connection to the Universal energy of Spirit. It facilitates meditation, hearing your intuition, and connection to the Divine.

TEA TREE

Tea Tree is a powerful releasing scent for clearing out mental and emotional stress. It supports the integration of new perspectives and encourages strength and clarity. A highly restorative oil, Tea Tree can clear your chakras and auric sphere. It's especially effective for bringing balance and harmony to the upper Third Eye and Crown Chakras.

YLANG YLANG

Ylang Ylang is an exotic floral scent associated with yin, or receptive, energy. It's connected to the Heart Chakra and is known to reduce stress, tension, and anxiety. This calming and soothing property helps move through feelings of resistance as they arise when releasing and surrendering habits and attachments.

Room & body clearing mist

I highly recommend clearing your space and body from stagnant, unwanted, or negative energy before performing any ritual. A common, traditional method for doing this is to use sage or sweetgrass smoke cleansing bundles. However, it's not always possible or desirable to use fire, matches, and smoke for your clearing.

Instead, you can create a Clearing Mist with water mixed with essential oils possessing these same energy cleaning properties.

Once mixed up, spritz your personalized Clearing Mist whenever it's needed. If you're clearing a physical space, remember to focus on moving the energy in the corners of the room by directing your Clearing Mist there.

If you're working to clear your physical and energetic body, try two different methods to see which one you prefer. First, you can send several sprays into the air in front of your body and then step through the mist. Alternately, you can hold your hand out and spray your body directly, taking care to avoid your eyes.

Sacred body anointing oil

This is one of my favorite ways to incorporate scent in my daily life. I combine one or two essential oils with a carrier oil such as jojoba or avocado. You can mix the oils into a bottle or simply put the jojoba oil in one hand and add a few drops of the essential oil to blend only what you need each time.

Once you've selected the scent you're working with and mixed it with the carrier oil, you can apply it to your pulse points. You can apply the oil at touchpoints throughout the day, such as first thing in the morning, after a shower, or just before bed. The most common pulse points are the neck, wrists, and behind the knees. Besides these points, you can also anoint yourself with scented oil in alignment with your chakras.

When working with manifestation energy, a powerful place to apply your oil is just below your belly button at your Sacral Chakra. This is your creative power center, and applying anointing oil here activates and nourishes your sacred connection to the Divine.

Moon bliss bath

Enhance the healing power of your bath by using mineral salts infused with essential oil. On its own, oil will bead up and float on the surface of the water. When mixed with salt, the oils will be slowly released throughout the water.

In addition to carrying the scent, salt has its own spiritual and healing properties. Mineral salt is highly grounding and purifying. It carries away unwanted energy you're ready to release, allowing you to let go of attachments and make room to manifest abundance.

Salt is associated with both the Water and Earth elements, making it a powerful tool for creating balance in your subtle emotional and energy bodies. As an Earth element, salt is linked to the health and well-being of your Root Chakra.

To make your own blissful moon bath, take a scoop of salt in a bowl or your hand and sprinkle with a few drops of the oil you've chosen to work with. For the salt, you can look for either Epsom salt or an unscented mineral bath salt. Mix the salt together lightly and allow the essential oil to soak into the salts. Then sprinkle them into the warm bath water.

As you soak in the water's warmth, set an intention for the scent, salt, and water to help you to shed negative energy, limiting beliefs, and old patterns that no longer serve you. Visualize this process unfolding gently for your highest and best good.

Candle blessing

Lightly rubbing a candle with a chosen essential oil and then burning it all the way down is like sending up a prayer to Spirit. The flame of the candle symbolizes the sacred light of your soul and connection to the Divine.

Start by infusing your intention into the candle by mindfully covering it with a very thin layer of your chosen essential oil. Speak your prayer of intention over the candle as you do so, and then light it when you're able to let it safely burn through. Small chapel candles or tea lights are perfect for this, as they typically last only a few hours.

As the flame reaches up to the sky, it carries your intentions for either manifesting or releasing. For added effectiveness, you could repeat this same ritual for two or three nights in a row as an expression of your commitment to realizing your desired outcome.

If you're interested in expanding beyond single note essential oils, try these blends in your sprays, baths, or body oils. I intuitively mix my oils, adding more of each one until the balance feels and smells right. If you add just a few drops at a time, you can easily adjust the scent until you find your unique sweet spot.

SACRED SCENT BLENDS

Abundance - Ginger, Jasmine

Compassion - Rose, Bergamot, Orange

Divine Feminine - Ylang Ylang, Rose

Grounding - Cedar, Sandalwood

Meditation - Sandalwood, Tea Tree

Momentum - Ginger, Cypress, Ylang Ylang

Peace - Bergamot, Sandalwood, Rose

Self-Love - Rose, Ylang Ylang, Bergamot

Sensuality - Jasmine, Ylang Ylang, Patchouli

Transformation - Cedar, Rose

FURTHER READING

Ariadne's Thread, Shekinah Mountainwater (2018) Echo Point Books & Media

Finding the Deep River Within: A Woman's Guide to Recovering Balance and Meaning in Everyday Life, Abby Seixas (2007) Jossey-Bass

New Moon Astrology: The Secret of Astrological Timing to Make All Your Dreams Come True, Jan Spiller (2001) Bantam

Rachel Pollack's Tarot Wisdom: Spiritual Teachings and Deeper Meanings, Rachel Pollack (2008) Llewellyn Publications

Sacred Space: Clearing and Enhancing the Energy of Your Home, Denise Linn (1995) Wellspring/Ballantine

Tarot for Your Self: A Workbook for the Inward Journey, Mary Greer (2019) Weiser Books

The Spiral Dance: A Rebirth of the Ancient Religion of the Goddess: 20th Anniversary Edition, Starhawk (1999) HarperOne

ACKNOWLEDGMENTS

This book is truly a divine collaboration and was nourished by a circle of incredible souls.

There are so many women who I've had the good fortune to howl, create, write, and play with: Melinda, Wendy, Cristin, Patricia, Nicola, Stephanie, Laura, and Sara. Each of you greets life with passion, grit, throaty laughter, and deep reverence. I'm grateful to each and every one of you for our sisterhood and friendship.

To all my ancestors and the women I haven't named, this book is for you, in honor of you, and because of you.

I want to honor and acknowledge my gratitude for Abby Seixas, who trained me in her beautiful Deep River circle work. Thank you for writing your book and inspiring me to go deeper, to listen, and to slow down with compassion and connection.

For my sister, who has helped me be more true to myself, more loving, accepting, and compassionate. I'm so glad we're on this wild ride together.

And for my sweet boys, the two lights in my life who keep my heart filled with love and laughter. Mama does this work for all of us.

To my husband, thank you for loving and supporting me unconditionally, and for bringing music, magical forests, and adventure into our lives.

I love you to the moon and back.

ABOUT THE AUTHOR

Leah Kent is a writer, book coach, and book designer. She helps radiant, creative visionaries bring their books and sacred body of work to life.

Leah supports heart-centered creatives, experts, and entrepreneurs to write and publish books that share their message, establish their thought-leadership, and expand their impact and visibility. Her clients have affectionately called her a Book Midwife and a Literary Witch of Wonder.

Through private book coaching and her small group programs, she helps writers stay inspired, focused, and connected to their greatest strengths throughout the creative process.

To learn more, visit leahkent.net

www.ingramcontent.com/pod-product-compliance
Lightning Source LLC
Chambersburg PA
CBHW071417070526
44578CB00003B/591